Sugar
&
Heartmeat

C.R. Andrews

Cover and interior photos courtesy of
Heather Andrews except where otherwise noted.

ISBN-13: 978-1499201239
ISBN-10: 1499201230

DEDICATION

This book is dedicated to my father, who received every
first draft and got me to write again.

.

CONTENTS

FOREWORD

For those of you who are used to my songwriting you will find this to be quite different. Unlike most, I generally know ahead of time if I'm going to write a song, a poem, a story, or none of the above. Some of these qualify as "none of the above." I am always hesitant to call it poetry. Generally this is what I write when I'm not creative enough to write a song. . . which is often. Then again, poetry is subjective. Despite what they like to teach you in college there really are no rules. Walk through the downtown of any metropolis and you are sure to find giant sculptures of a bean or a 30 foot spoon and it qualifies as priceless art. So if a giant spoon is art then I suppose I can call this poetry.

I write because I need to write. I don't do it for you. I don't do it for critics. I don't do it for acknowledgement. And if you believe that then I've got a bridge to sell you. All writers write for themselves first but it is always directed at someone. Someone we love or someone we hate. That is the myth about writers. . . that we don't care what people think. The writing really isn't validated until it touches someone. The selfish part of writing is true in one aspect. I'm not going to change anything in the hopes of appealing to someone. If you get something out of it without me having to try and affect you then I have succeeded. If you pick one line out of this book that means something to you then I'm going to call it a win. Perhaps it inspires you to put a pen to paper yourself and not care what comes out. Remember, anything is poetry as long as you are honest. Either way, it isn't a giant fucking spoon. . .

this is not a poem

i thought that i would write you a poem.
not that you asked
or that you would even want one
But this isn't exactly a poem
and i am not exactly a poet

i wasted most of my good words years ago
some were received and some left outside to die
either way they all ended up wandering the streets
after the rain washed away the scent
of those they were created for
they just haven't ever managed to find their way back
home
i left the door open for them
i left the porchlight on
Sometimes I think I hear them
scratching at the window
or shivering in the crook of the tree outside
sometimes when the cat cries at nothing at all
i think that maybe he sees them
and he is trying to tell me.
then i remember he is a fucking cat
and i am not a fucking poet

i know you deserve more than this
this was supposed to be a love poem after all
i am supposed to be moved to create something
something to bring you over to my longing and my
disgrace
i owe you that much
something new
something new because your beauty is new
and shrouded
and wet

you tell me that you want me and i want to call you a
madwoman
you say that you need me and i want to punish you
instead of running straight into your arms and your bed
all I can give you is words
and they still haven't come home

tap tap tap...

I suppose i could sit here and spin some indulgent
metaphor for your beauty
i could talk about your perfect white skin and your eyes
how i shake sometimes because i think i can feel it or
how i can always feel your eyes ignoring all that i think is
ugly and wretched

i can smell the kitchen and the morning air as you cook
breakfast
i am hanging your pictures
i am teaching your children about the evils in the world
we are adopting a kitten with one good eye

but yet I sit here
i lie here
with nothing to offer you
just leftover words
as each morning i wake up and
reach out to touch the dawn
which i have a thousand times
mistaken for your mouth

but i am not a fucking poet.

<u>i used to write</u>

There was a time when I used to write.
And actually, looking back,
I think I was pretty damn good at one time.
And I used to write much more creatively than this drivel.
I had even developed my own distinctive style.
It was a bit similar to E.E. Cummings.
Then again,   (maybe)
                              i   just
                              copied
                                      him

                                   completely.

Grace

Let us make no affectations upon these days
let us not make trivial
the journey to your flesh.
Perform with your tranquil lips
a litany of kisses upon these hands
which with avarice
concede to every motion.
as I touch you with my mind
receive me

just once,
just kiss me

The Unicorn

you make me want to write
to write from
a place of beauty
instead of always
from the darkness
It is a place I can't find
a place I do not know
but I am making my way
back again
slowly
feeling through the darkness
past the memories
of the whores
and the false
and the weak
and the hidden

with each day
I gain the courage
to push them aside
to not look back
to not listen to their words
I will not accept
their acts of martyrdom

I will just move
towards your beauty
where I can be free again
where I can give everything
while you ask for nothing

I will keep moving
into your broken smile
to disappear between your legs

and have my hands
strangled by your hair

I will let myself want again
I will abandon everything again

just once more

<u>because</u>

it is because i love
you
    that a hundred nights
may fall finally, (priceless)
into my palms

it is because you may
love me
    that purpose for all
monuments of stone
throughout time
might reveal suddenly
(to) this mind

it is because i love
you
    that each strand of your
hair...
a trail for pilgrimage
upon where i might
make worth of my heart

it is because you may
love me
      that my hands
forsake the flesh
of any other offering

it is because i love
you
    that my body would cringe
upon the touch of other
than your hands

when the grain is deeply
absorbed
and the moon lets my body be
to drink the one truth

it is because you would not
love
    me.

5:56

the smell of death
gets into your clothes
and your skin
it hits your face like
walking into a wall
of rotting meat
and fermenting piss

the smell is there
long before the moment comes
you smell it coming
you smell the hopelessness
if you have never experienced it
you will
someday
we all do

you don't have to actually
be around the body
after the moment comes
you will absorb the death
before it arrives
the smell is there
the moment is coming
it hits you in waves
you smell it as soon as you
walk off of the elevator
but in the room you can taste it

it will be all over your clothes
in the morning
it will be in everything you eat
everything you drink

it will sit in the roots
of your hair
it lines your nose

I see myself there
I wonder who would decide.
I wonder if it would be difficult.
If I could hear anyone
and would they even talk to me.
If they did would I even know
that anyone was there?

13 days

in 13 days i will have you
you will be mine
if only for a moment
if only for a night
or a few hours
all that matters is
that you will be mine
we will cast off the
rest of the world
no longer own any pain
or longing
there will be nothing but
you and I

this is why we stay alive
so that in-between the madness
we can finally feel solace
in mercy
and love

<u>I was alive</u>

I was alive.
i was alive for a moment

but it was supposed to be too late
i grew to accept that it was too late
it was the only thing i knew
eventually we will accept anything we are dealt
no matter the futility or the struggle
we simply stop the struggling
and lie limp and submit to the things
that we think we deserve

then there was you
damn you.
you and your voice
your words of redemption
damn you for believing in me
damn you for making me believe

and then you were gone
and i slipped back
where i belong
back behind the wall
under the rock
back to the broken nights
and the robotic days

I loved you for demanding nothing

then cursed you when
you insisted on having it all
even though you claimed
to know what we were

and then you returned

and I am alive
again I am alive
and it only took a moment
it only took a night
a touch
a breath
a look
a kiss
a drink
a word

in an instant
our time was fulfilled
and I knew who I was
where I belonged
where you belonged
once again I was human
finally my hands are strong
my back is straight
my voice is true
my breath is calm
again I am alive
again I am a man

The Secret Of Life

Sometimes in the middle of the night
among the banality of the infomercials
one of these cretins inspires an epiphany
the get rich quick guy told me
that you'll never get anywhere laboring for someone else
It's true
There is no money in service.
Waitress, clerk, driver,
mover, secretary.
He's right. It applies to
every one of them.
Ironic that the only exception to the rule
is this whore I just gave my
last 50 dollars to.

They've got it made.

<u>divinity</u>

Many recent evenings
my thoughts have turned to you
and i have to confess
they were somewhat lustful

those moments when
i am urged
by a ceremony of flesh
the history of
your wounded sex
revealed and
perverse fingers trace
a long path
each digit whispering your name

let me drink from you
indulge
in your intoxicating skin
ascending to meet my own amazement
in the burning folds of divinity.

<u>23 years old</u>

at some point
things hold no joy
any longer

everything is an effort

there is no distinction
between chores, errands, or hobbies.
I feel I should
build something,
fix something,
cook something.
create.
advance my life.

eventually you realize
that you are either as
complete as you can be
or accept that you never will be.

We are always moving
forward or backward
and eventually you come
to the point where there
is no distinction between the two.
Your passions will
become pointless.
Things that made you charming
eccentric, and fascinating
are now outdated.

It is different when
you are 23.
You can be a struggling artist

or musician.
But 15 years later you are
just pathetic.
Now you are just an old man
keeping the company of ghosts
You aren't even washed up.
To be washed up you had
to have been successful at some point.

Even worse is to be
a writer or a poet.
A 23 year old poet or writer
is accepted
it is sexy and intriguing.
It will get you women
It will get you free drinks
and a bed for the night

And for some reason
at that age people associate it
with intelligence
passion
drive
and an open future.

But pushing 40
it is no longer admirable.
it is barely interesting

Now it is time to simply accept
You won't write the
next great novel
you are not the
undiscovered poet.
you are not the
undiscovered anything.

You have nothing left
to be discovered.

You are a cog.
You are part of the machine
and a machine
of minor importance.
The machine will take you
and you can't resist.
You will tell yourself
it is a good life
consider yourself successful
and justify your decisions.

But you continue
to write
to dream
While others continue
to admire you
Tell you how much
you have grown.
They are all so proud
But you are just
a fraud like

all of the rest.
People admire
complacency
and the norm
and now that is all you are.

This

this.
this tepid vacant evening
and my words
nothing in the palms of the rain

thoughts of your porcelain flesh
visions of the eyes that would mean
to enclose me,
into your fingertips
into your own thrusting lips.

this.
this commencement of our flesh
raising above your beauty
greeting your scent on my lips.
writhing thighs
across my hips like a cricket.

this.
this control you have abandoned
until you are ready to receive
me spilled
into-upon-across

You.

<u>I will</u>

I will give you everything
i will hand wash your clothes
i will fix the stuck window
i will read to your child
i will make breakfast
i will behave around your parents
i will stop smoking
i will tolerate your ex-husband
i will listen to
what happened in your day
i will hold your purse
while you shop
i will let you cry
i will let you have all the blankets
i will give you the last cupcake

and all i need is for you
to
let me

<u>know this</u>

On this day, my dear
know this.

You, longer than aware beneath my skin
taunting each nerve with your mere existence
when finally I washed my jaded breath into
your grace
a lucid dream in your deepest eyes
your words covered me.
But now these drowning fingers do toil
on each wasted verse,
unrequited lips gaze
across your skin of a perfect porcelain doll.
I know now it is an epitaph
for pointless efforts to be left wounded
more deeply than a thousand Caesars

Yet I moved forward with trembling steps
only to break down in lost idolatry
your beauty forever unowned by me.
I, with imminent destruction from my own Iago
(but he whispers truths).
And still nothing is learned.
But all is known

My words are now spent.
what more can i compare
to your mouth, eyes, and breasts
or to my disgrace?

conversations: part 1

If you were so unhappy
then why did you
marry him
in the first place?

"He was the first man who
didn't try to rape me
or put his hands all over me."

why did you stay?

"He was the only man
who ever really turned me on."

How?

". . . by existing."

<u>the last drink I ever took</u>

whenever you pour
the last glass out of
the bottle it always ends up
being more than you
thought it was
after pouring singles or
doubles all night
that last glass
always ends up being about
4 or 5 fingers
and I'll be damned
if I wasn't going to finish it.

"let's go to bed baby"
she said gently as
she walked towards me with
more tenderness than she should.
she ran her hand
up my arm and looked
into my eyes but
not pleading and not sad
just accepting

she kissed me gently and
ran her lips up to my
ear
"Just come to bed with me baby."
as she reached to the
glass in my hand

I almost let go but
then I tightened my grip and
it turned into a short struggle as
she tightened hers as well

and it jostled the glass and
whiskey splashed up the
side of the tumbler
and it poured down both of
our hands

and she never took her
lips away from my ear.

i backed my head away and
looked into her eyes
her eyes still not sorrowful
and without pity and
without disappointment.
 she never told me that
she thought i had enough
she never asked me to stop
not with her
eyes or her lips

my hand dripping with 18 year old
whiskey i raised it up and pulled it back
my lips quivering and my breath
rapidly increasing as i stood
motionless and stared at her with
cold hollow eyes as i clutched
the glass

her expression never changed
there was no fear in her eyes
she just moved back
to me
she wrapped her arms around
my waist and kissed me as my lips
slowly parted and muttered the beginning
of a thought that hadn't even been formed.

then she moved her
lips to my ear once again

"Shhhh. . .
then share it with me lover"

i stood silent...motionless
She looked hard right through
my eyes and wrapped her tiny hand around mine
that held the glass.
i went limp as she moved
the glass to her lips

I watched as we held the
glass and she took the
entire content into her mouth.
she winced and her
eyes leaked tears and as she coughed
with a slight smile
It seemed like half of it
had sprayed out of her mouth and
ran down her lips and chin
and neck
and down to her breasts.

my body relaxed and I felt as
if i took my first calm breath of the evening
as she took the glass and put it on
the piano then once again
she kissed me
and i could taste the whiskey on her lips
the soft texture of them along with
the sting of the whiskey
was erotic and humbling
and shameful.

I pulled up
her skirt and took her
right there on the piano

after that she took
me to our bed and
i held her
I once again tried to speak as
she put her finger calmly to my lips
silencing me once again

"Did you really think I was going to give up on you?"

always

you are the manifestation
of all the dreams
i couldn't remember
you are the cold sweat that
wakes me at night
i have found a meaning
and a purpose
in your arms
i continue to exist
because you love me
because you have
accepted my limitations
because there are no
hidden intentions

in spite of distance or time
or what has faded between us
i will always belong to you
and you will
always belong to me

martyr

I used to be your special guest
Because of you now all the rest
Will be nothing more than tainted flesh
To fill my hollow baited chest
With the apathetic webs that you taught me.
They shall know the cold as I
Know mistrusting twisted eyes
Not understanding their own cries
A rotten decayed goodbye
And the many other deaths that you brought me.

All the fools will think they know
As a horrid lust begins to grow
They will know that they are weak and slow
With burning pride from down below
And I will snuff it out without even breathing.
No concern of who shall fall
I will not respond to a hopeless call
These empty insects they will crawl
Up my rusted fermented wall
And I will crush them when I complete my feeding.

For now I am truly dead
I've seen the cruelty inside your head
I've felt my body soaked in red
Bled my sainthood for that man in your bed
This unattached bliss it does not suit you.
And as I scavenge this death with bleeding tongue
To lick the scraps in deserted scum
Swallowing my wretched fate to come
Your flesh under another comes undone
With not a thought of what I will go through.

And you will not see me as I waste away
From your misspent affections of yesterday
And this vile eternal game we play
From an estranged wasteland where I refuse to stay
You will not even know my final breath.
You will smell my body in dirt and wood
If a tear happens to fall and I think it should
As I've done the only thing I could
Enslaved to a devotion that did no good
Which I can only break in a martyred death.

you are

You are my breath
and my life

My most depraved
and most beautiful thoughts

You are my every step
My every movement
My every gesture

You are the reason that writers write,
singers sing,
sculptors sculpt.

You are the dreams of fantasies
the fantasies of dreams

You are the hopes of wishes
and the wishes of hope

You are the sun that
touches my face
through the curtains at dawn

You are the reflection
in the eyes of my unborn child

You are the first rose of summer
and the last leaf of fall

you are the softest pillow
and the warmest blanket

You are the first taste

of the greatest feast
and the last drop of the best whiskey.

You are what every
man has searched for
but only
I have found.

Leonard Cohen

Last night I cried
but not how you want me to
Last night I cried for Leonard Cohen
I did not cry for you

I remembered the Sisters of Mercy
and all the things they do
I gave thanks to Leonard Cohen
and there was nothing left for you

Last night, I dreamed of Marianne
and the Future
and the guests that have come through
I dreamed I was in the Chelsea Hotel
and in none of it was you

Tonight I am scaling the tower of song
to my secret life and mirrored room
I drank with Hank Williams
and we did not drink to you

Tonight I left you waiting
for tears you never knew
because I only cry for Cohen
and this is not for you.

I was ready

You are vain.

a cruel and
frightened
child.

I thought you were ready,
you are not ready.

I was ready.

I was ready
from the beginning.

But this requires
the concern of two.

you want to be close,
to support,
to care,
and not need the others.
you want to create life
you want to create *our* life

Unfortunately,
you promise this
in the same breath as when
you contend you can promise nothing
and that

your thoughts may change tomorrow.

everything you say has to
have a disclaimer

that allows you to stay free
or to defend your future actions.
you are more enamored
with your fear of relationships
than the effort to grow

I am sad
but I have lost nothing

sadness gives way to sorrow,

loss sustains them both.

<u>my Dad is better than your dad</u>

my dad is better than
your dad.

my dad can kick
your dad's ass.
Then he would kick your ass too.

and then go listen to some Sondheim.

you just got the shit kicked out of you
by an old man who drinks microbrews
and listens to Sondheim.

"Tons O' Fun"...
that's what he would call me.
it's really not that bad if you had seen me
i was a fat little bastard.
Of course now I'm just an older fat bastard.

Compared to my friends
 it was a goddamn Normal Rockwell childhood
My friends have fathers that are drunks,
degenerates, fiends, strangers, or just plain dead.
At least he was always there.

He was there when I lost my first love.
And the second.
He was there for the recitals.
He made me eat my eggs.
He gave me sips of his beer.
He taught me paint, drywall, and plumbing.
Although for Christmas he gave me
skis instead of an AT-AT
he also gave me my first book of

Cohen, Dali, and Cummings.

He was there for the overdose.
He was there for the bleeding hands
and the cigarette burns.
He stepped on rusty nails for me.
He brought the camera to every pointless thing I ever did.

my dad is better than your dad.
He can run faster than your dad.
And he knows more than your dad.
He has shoulders like Johnny Weissmuller.
He speaks like Atticus Finch.
My dad could take control of the Enterprise.
My dad is Shakespeare,
Hannibal Lecter,
and Batman.

My dad thinks Chuck Norris is a pussy.

My dad has that serious old man grip
like a mechanic.
The kind where they grab your arm
and it scares the shit out of you and
you could swear they are lifting you
3 feet off of the ground.
That is one thing I did not inherit.
I ended up with my mother's hands.

My dad climbs a rope without using his legs.
My dad can park a station wagon in a motorcycle space.
My dad can drink more Jameson than you.
My dad can sing along with
every Bread song ever written.

then he would kick your dad's ass.

Photograph by Sara Andrews

there was a time

There was a time
when I was beautiful.

the women
wanted my hands and
would covet my words
and it would begin with forgiveness
before it was earned

somehow

you still want me.

to complete something
in your life
be it lovely or depraved.
And you have accepted my soul
before it is saved.

but I am selfish
and I am cruel
I am faithless
I am gray
I have turned to clay and
have forgotten how to bleed.

you liked my kiss

I left from your grace
walked the damp streets
my clothes spent
lips ragged and torn
your smell owned my skin

every virtue lost
all vows broken
there was no restraint
restraint was never even
considered around you

the wanting burned
maybe it was just lust
maybe it was more.
But however treacherous
or wrong our movements,
the need exists

You said you liked my kiss
but I can't describe
your lips breaking
upon

how I trembled

You said you liked what I do to you
but I felt my body and
wilted hands struggle
with the task

we must not touch again
our hearts cannot be burdened

for if but once more I felt
your mouth, your breath,
your smell against me

i might be forced to love thee.

what i want

It is uncertain
it is too soon
it is illogical
it is unsafe
it is not the time
it is not the place
the wounds are still fresh
as i still try
to figure out
where they came from

It is wrong
it is unconventional
it is embarrassing
it is insane
i am too young
i am too old
i am too broken
and she is too scared
and this could continue
indefinitely

but even with all of this
i will jump into the abyss
into the fray.
I have abandoned everything
that is rational
just for the chance to feel
her thin fingers run
down my arm.

Just to see her in my chair
to see her petting my cats

to see her asleep on the couch.
To hear the slightest movements
of her body in the water
as i pass by the bathroom door.

just for the chance
to push her soft blond hair
behind her ear
as she tells me about her day.
To be able to come up from behind
and kiss the base of her neck
while she cooks dinner.
Finally alone
Lost in the subtle
and exhausted touch of each other.

To make her feel safe
adored
and loved.

this is what i want
and i will take a chance
just for that chance.

How easily I might forget
========================

How easily I might forget
if I might be enraptured in your flesh
of my ill-willed tongue,
and dignity thrown amiss.
How easily I might deny
if I knew your beauty
the scar of truth, if engulfed in your kiss.

an unattainable feast
An undeniable lust
now only a forgotten drink.
Sacrificed to childlike trust
was each grain of pride,
now struggling to vengeance

How easily I might give
          (if tangled in your hair)
unselfish gifts of praise from what little lives on
.........below.
How easily I might forget
-if buried in your flesh-
(if i knew Your beauty,
'tis all i wish to know).

Jameson Inn

we will continue to try
continue to justify
these mornings
the hours that
i traveled hours for

but we know what this is
we know what we
want it to be
we know exactly what
it cannot and
will not be
but we will live in
these moments
on our wishes

i will continue to stare
when you ask me
what i am thinking
i will continue to say
"nothing."

i think you see the words
that i won't let escape
the words that i choke on
the words that make
my hands shake against you
I try to tell you with
the way i hold you against me

the way i receive your kiss
the way i trace every curve
of your face
and fall into this world

that you have given to me

then we will send each other
back to our lives
back to them
back to longing
and complicity
ours and theirs

but even years from now

i will never forget

sweet tea
and mornings
at the Jameson Inn

the dead unicorn

tonight i slew a unicorn
i ripped her horn
i flayed her from head to heel
i left her drawn and quartered
her beauty was too much for me
the legend was too real
i scalped her mane
i blinded her eyes
i burned her in the forest
nobody deserves this beauty
i killed her just as
i have destroyed
everything beautiful
that i have ever encountered
i left this beauty
and i will leave it for
no one else to find
i will bury her
i won't keep her captive
but i want no man to discover her
the legend will fade away
it will fade
with me

<u>bastard</u>

She never knew that I watched her
in the mornings.
As she dressed for work she always thought I was
always in a dead sleep.
But I was watching. I was watching her.
Watching her lithe body stumbling half awake
towards the shower.
This was one of the only ways I could view her body.
She wouldn't deliberately allow me to.
A green curtain hung where a bathroom door should be.
Under the curtain I could see her toes curl
against the cold tile.
She always slept in the same gray cotton shorts
and from under the curtain I would watch them fall
to the floor.
I could almost hear the sound of her slender arm
reaching to the faucet.
I hear the squeak of the old faucet stems.
The thump and the rumble of the water pressure being
released.
And I could even hear her holding back her hair. . .

This is one of the ways I would live
vicariously through inanimate objects
I was always jealous of that room.
The light of the vanity illuminating her body
The hours the mirror has been able to watch that face
And the water has explored more of her body
than I ever will
Sometimes the anger would grow as I heard the
water splashing against her skin and when it got to be
too much I would cover my face I would begin to
cry and force myself back into several
hours of unnecessary sleep.

I obsessed over every part of her.
I never knew from one moment to the next
what aspect of her
would entrance me next.
But it never really mattered,
I knew every part was one that I would never have.
At least not in the way I need it. I need too much.
I make slaves with my greed. Of myself and others
and the needs feel normal
Acceptable
For once I want to be viewed as I have viewed
others. . .as I have viewed her.
To obsess over me from time to time for no
apparent reason at all.
For no valid reasons.
Simply having the quality that draws her near.

All of my thoughts of her are endless
Limitless.
and useless.

And I watch her eyes as she speaks to me
I look for body language
A way to interpret it all.
She spouts out various phrases
"I love you."
"how was your day?"
"I'm making your favorite dinner."
But as I look to her mouth and watch
her small thin perfect lips
they always slowly form the same thing.
"You bastard. . . I loathe you."
and she has every right
I deserve
this.

come to me
--

you,
lady of confused adoration
stirring a typically reserved style
and dormant desire.

come to me,
some fragile evening
with your exact lips
and the sharp curves of your skin.

you,
A last hope
for redemption of my solitude
i offer to your hands
my remaining broken down breaths
left by wolves of misspent youth.

come to me,
some frozen evening
with your long pale flesh
and lazy confirming hair.

let me try
your searching stare
against your breast
and crawling downward
descending everywhere.

cats and dogs

I don't like people
very much but
most of the time I wish that
more of them were around.
i wonder sometimes if i
drove people away
or if i just
didn't want to deal
with them anymore

i suppose that is the same thing

generally people will betray
deceive
lie
and let you down
that is why i would rather be around animals.
I like animals better than people.
i like cats and dogs
and i like cats better
than dogs

my cats won't try to fuck my girlfriend.
my cat didn't have his
car parked outside of her house
as i howled at the moon
pounding a bloody hand against
the door of the foyer.
the cats don't care if i am
drunk or fat or irrational.
All they need is food and shelter
water and a belly rub.

people don't purr.

they are not entertained by an empty box
they don't play with my feet
through the blanket.
they aren't happy eating the same thing every day
they still want to be near you in spite of
how you feel about yourself.
cats will trust completely
unequivocally
shameless and egoless
they will always need me

once you have taken
them into your heart the
only world they feel the need to explore
is the one that you have created for them
for their comfort and their safety.
They actually appreciate your sacrifice

and they don't care where i have been
they are simply
glad that i am home

and all this will remain
until the day that they let me
know that they are ready to
die

and they even put that
in your hands.

D.T. Lott

Everything i ever needed to know I learned
from D.T. Lott.

It was a cold Chicago night...late on a Wednesday on
Sheffield avenue.
We got into his barely functional car with no heat.
Our dusty guitar cases held together with string and duct
tape in the back.
I raged about life and love until we pulled up to my
apartment.
He handed me a cassette and said "I think you're ready for
this."
It was called "The Heart of Saturday Night."

Once inside I dropped the dirty yellowed tape into the
deck it only took about 6 seconds.
The quick open and close of the hi-hat as the first
note...the subtle but defining jazz fill that follows and leads
to the first dissonant minor chord on what was clearly an
old upright bar piano.
I was sold.
Then the voice.
The voice that formed the rest of my life.

The next track started.

a Serenade.

The most perfect progression of flatted chords. It was
seamless. Then came the strings that

made my soul float.
It was the first time i realized that I was not alone.
And I owe it all to D.T. Lott.

Then I was ready for Cohen, Keats, Yeats, and Neruda.
My education never stopped.
We would drink coffee and tea...

(well I never drank tea)

We had grapes and whiskey. We talked about why there
were no tambourines in jazz. We named our imaginary
bands until settling on "Chip Whiskey and the Mojo
Crapshoot."
We laughed,
we read,
we strummed,
and sometimes we fought

"EMOTE!"

"What?"

"EMOTE!"

"I don't even know what the fuck that means!"

Of course he explained it to me in an overly animated and
almost threatening manner. He lunged at me, poked my
chest, grabbed me, and pontificated.

But all I saw was the threat; the insult.

And we did not speak for 2 years.

But eventually I learned. I knew what he meant and what
he demanded.
Talent didn't matter.
It was that feel...
The respect for the music. The honor of the words.

He was right.
He was always right.
And eventually it came to pass that we both learned what it was like to study without a friend.

We traveled from the Midwest to the south. We saw Graceland and we sang at the King's grave.
We both saw nothing but loneliness in the rooms and the halls. We were almost arrested in Cairo, Illinois by an overzealous redneck trooper.

He showed me New Orleans--the real New Orleans (Fuck Bourbon street). We got our to-go cups and we played guitar outside Le Petit. We walked across the brick roads as the giant cockroaches followed.
I met Roger. We had vodka and dry white toast in the morning as he performed an entire musical about Robin Hood.
I saw all the places that tourists would not dare to go. And there was nothing big or easy about any of it.

Years went by. He disappeared, he reappeared. Searching for something that could not be found.
The roads all around the world looked the same and they had all grown weary of being looked at.

He is jaded now, possibly insane. He learned too much and applies too much of it to himself.
And i cannot help him. We can no longer laugh or drink things away. We cannot find the meaning anymore. And i don't have the words. I can't offer the words he used to offer to me so long ago. I learned nothing. Everything he taught me are things I cannot give back.

The student has failed.

these are the times

these are the times that matter
when you discover
that you don't matter
your time is gone
you had your moment in the sun

and it was good

it was glorious

you were beautiful
you got drinks from strangers
from the girl with glasses
who wore a broken vow
for a tattoo

you remember the day
when you touched people
you made them feel

they found meaning
in your work
that you never even
intended in the first place

that is when you were important
when you meant something
when you weren't trying
now you have to
force it
struggle to be
that person again
find the words that will
announce your presence

words and sounds
that demand attention
and respect

but you don't have them anymore
you are a face in the crowd
a master of nothing
and a slave to mediocrity
you will not be remembered
you will be less
than forgotten
you have affected nothing
the world will continue
to die
with or without you
there are no roads that care
if you have gazed upon them
there are no arches
that need you to pass through them
no souls you need to touch
no flesh that needs your embrace
your longing is not needed
or wanted
you will remain incomplete

you are done

I have a woman waiting

I have a woman waiting
she goes about her life
but she waits
she waits for me
she waits as I struggle
as i fumble
as i try to make sense
of a new life

there is a woman waiting
she is kind and new
and a stranger
yet she knows
she knows what i am
i've never seen her eyes
but i feel her watching me
watching
waiting

i have a woman waiting
whom with every day
her patience grows as great
as her beauty
i don't know why she waits
but she has another life for me
another world
between her thin fingers

there is a woman waiting
i've not even held her hand
but i can feel it
against my chest
i feel her fingers
across my lips

just as I can smell her hair
just as i can feel
the small of her back
in the palm of my hand

I have a woman waiting
i want to keep her there
locked up
until the day when
we can release each other
when i remember
that alone is just
alone

this woman is waiting
and with everything that
i don't know
i already want to abandon
myself to her
to take her
to claim her as mine

i have a woman waiting
and i need her there
waiting

please love...

wait for me

<u>beauty</u>

there are times
when she thinks
she is not beautiful
she waits for me to reject her
I look in the mirror
and I see the lines grow deeper
the bags and the color
the weight of years
that have ravaged my face and body
i wonder if she does the same thing
i wonder if she is doing it now
Then i hold her picture in my hand
i stare at it
i study it and fall into her
and i wonder what she sees

I will make her feel beautiful
she will see herself
through my eyes
she will learn the power
that she holds
in every movement of her body
how the sound of her voice
humbles me
The way she can
turn me into a child
with a look or a word

She wants me to command her
even though just the thought

of her touch
can crumble me into dust
and i will let her

Even as she surrenders
I let her beauty crush me.
And i will guide her
i will fall into that beauty
that she has put into my hands

and i swear to G-d
she will know love.

1-R

sometimes I wonder
how we survived there
without freezing
or going mad
but those were some of
the best days of my life

we made it work.
1 room,
3 bachelors,
2 cats,
1 television
and for a while
the same woman

it was a time when smokers and
non-smokers could live together
in perfect harmony.
there were no iPods
no tablets
we had no internet
no smartphones
not even cell phones.
that's right...
we shared the same land line.
We took turns with dinner
...when we had dinner
sometimes that only involved a trip
down the block for booze
and some hamburger helper

somehow we were never
in each other's way
one of us could be in solitude

just 4 feet away
and all was right
that is how you know
a real friend
they let you sit at
the other end of the room
and fucking lose your shit
in silence
they just stand by and make sure
that you don't go
the other way

when you go that other way
they pause
they step in but
do it without movement
without actions
without words

my fist through the glass
muffled the room
i felt the stares
but i didn't stare back
yeah...
this was a new level
of losing my shit

but they didn't react
at least not deliberately
but they were making decisions
they were discussing it
as only men could
silently
with looks
nods
maybe

a grunt
this is what a woman will never
understand or know
how to do

I pulled a bottle from under the sink
and announced my departure
with a slamming door
and a trail of blood.
sometimes you just
leave someone be.
sometimes the most powerful sign of love
is when you do
nothing at all
Distance can be just as affectionate
as an embrace.
sometimes you just need to stay away
sometimes all you need
is to have been
seen

they know.
they don't force you to talk it out
they just keep an eye out
watch for that time
that one night
when enough is enough
when they show love
by letting you know that they are done
that you are done
and it doesn't need to be discussed.
that is what men do.

And enough was enough
enough was a phone call
enough involved Chicago PD

EMTs
restraints
puddles of blood
a mop
a father knocking on the door

it was a room shared with the biggest
blackest crackhead motherfucker
you can imagine.
He screamed all night.
my only respite came from the shrink.
If you have never heard a Chinaman
scream out the words "crazy" or
"schizophrenic" then you are really missing out.

discharged with the same
blood-stained clothes
i came in with
and a bus token

now i was the crazy fuck in
the back of the bus
the one that people judged
the one you write stories about
the one you recall when
you talk about the person that
you never want to be
the one you wonder
"what happened to him?"
and also the type that nobody
gives a shit about
the one you look away from

it was humiliating

and liberating

and empowering.

i finally made it home
no questions asked
a few hugs and smiles
actually not even that.
it didn't matter
we didn't need to talk it out
we didn't need to hug it out

this is what men do.

everything was known
everything was understood

they already knew what
they already knew why
they certainly knew who

and they knew what mattered.
to have
been
seen.

"So,
Motherfuckers. . .
what do you want to do to tonight?"

<u>brown hair</u>

There is a single thin
white
cigarette butt
wedged under the bridge of
a dollar-store beanbag
ashtray

menthol

each time i empty it
it just stays there
hanging on

that is the only reminder.

i've purged my home
of everything else
the evidence is gone
the memories are there but
nothing to invoke them

i tell them they are not welcome
that I have a new life now
this is my home
and it is the way
i want it
the furniture is where i want
the piano is now in the living room
there are no tampons
under the sink

no toast crumbs
no dirty dishes
there are no long brown hairs

in the carpet
or inside my socks

there is also nothing in the oven
there is no perfume in the air
nobody to help me to bed
nobody is singing in the bathtub
there is no laughter across the hall

and there is not a single long brown hair to be found

<u>fucking poetry</u>

one rarely asks for a poem
it spoils the surprise and the pleasure
of receiving one
if it should poke its head through the door

how words find their way back home
isn't the issue at all
what's important is
you left the porch light on
the screen door open
and they knew it was time to come home

and they did come home

whether you are or are not
a fucking poet
is irrelevant

you have written a fucking poem
and it is fucking poetry

(from Dad- 2/28/2012)

goodbye

"Where are you going?"

- "I don't know."

"Are you coming back?"

- "No."

"Can I visit you?"

- "No."

"Will I see you again?"

- "No."

"Will I hear from you again?"

- "No."

"So now what?"

-"Goodbye."

-----click-----

Where are you now old friend?

<u>summer</u>

It was June
the first time I saw her
even from a distance I could see
she was awkward
uncomfortable
as if she was in the middle
of a crowd for the first time
in her life.

She was tall and
she slouched a bit.
Everything was pink from
head to toe and she was
so adorably
out of place.

There were the initial periods
of silence
trying to make idle chatter
but it was never
uncomfortable

As we walked I finally
just reached out and took her hand
she made a content little
squeaking noise and
wrinkled her nose
grinning at me.
We walked and swung our arms
hand in hand
like clueless schoolchildren
smitten with puppy love
walking around the playground
during recess.

I think I was already
in love at that moment.
I never stood a chance,
not with her.
every touch and
every word and
every kiss from her from
that day forward just made me
dig in deeper
give in deeper.
There was no turning back and
I never wanted to. This was it.
I might have been in charge but
she owned me
and I'm not sure that she ever knew.

She watched everything that I did
as if it was all new
like a child amazed at
every sight and every moment
being so new and thrilling.
I was all that mattered
in her world
and my world knew only her
one that now could only exist
because she existed.

We were both wounded and
damaged to levels that
might never heal
and buried so deep
that we became them.
But together there was
no fear
or shame
and I judged nothing.

I just want to know
that look again
the eyes that saw nothing
but good
the embrace that
wiped away all of the ugliness
of the world.

I want to be able
to feel my arm relaxed again
with my palm
sweating nervously
just like
that clueless child
once again.

she is young

she is young
they said
says who?
i said
says all
they said
i don't care
i said
be cautious
they said
why?
i said
she is young
they said
is that all?
i said
it is wrong
they said
but why?
i said
it just is
they said
it is love
i said
you're a fool
they said

yes but she is still mine
i said

<u>the end</u>

Your eyes would change color
when you said
my name
you would tremble
and make all the sounds
that only i could hear
when i called you my little girl.
Your voice would dance up my arms
through my neck
tighten my jaw
and constrict around me
so much youth
and beauty that has
found its way into my home
and into my bed
and so unceremoniously
has come to an end

<u>memories</u>

i burned it all, yet
now all i wish
is for something with
the scent of you,
to cover up
the stench of
ashes

<u>one more day</u>

one more day
just one more day and
i'll do the dishes
one more day and
i'll clean those cobwebs off the wall
i'll do the laundry and
clean the vomit from the carpet
one more day and
i'll make that doctor's appointment
i'll get the oil changed and
rake up the leaves
just one more day and
i'll start on that novel
i'll work on that hit record
i'll start working out
one more day and
i'll cut down to a pack a day
i'll quit hard liquor and
sleep normal hours
just one more day and
she will finally see that her
life is worse without me
she will come running back with
tears in her eyes
one more day and she
will beg me to forgive her
beg for me to take her back and
go back to how things were
just one more day and
i will say this same shit again

liar

you were right.
they were all right
they are still right
there is nothing left here
you needed me to be strong
but it takes two
you moved on
you did it
quickly
you did it
easily
and without shame or regret
you can't have it both ways
you aren't allowed to
keep me in your life.
I have been your lover
I have been your martyr
and you wanted neither
I am done thinking you care
I am done comforting your guilt
you made your choice
you already let them choose.
and I just can't
believe you.

Not one
fucking
word.

J

just because
it doesn't mean
everything
doesn't mean that it
has to mean
nothing.
sometimes you
just need
to fill the void.

hands.
or lips.
or a lock of hair.
the scent of different shampoo
or lotion
or the natural scent
of different flesh.
something that reminds us that
we aren't the only ones like this but
in that moment are
all that matter.

something different to linger
in the air
or on our clothes
or on the pillow case.
something that makes us forget
what we see in the mirror.
makes us forget
what someone else sees.
to transform us back
from the beast that they
have turned us into.

there doesn't have to be a future.
what matters is
there is no past.
we never had the chance
to destroy each other.
it probably couldn't last
and is far from perfect.

But isn't it still worth a kiss?

<u>every other night</u>

When it is finally dark
When the cats have gone to bed
When my night has long since ended
When the last of the bottle is gone
When I've made it through one more day
When I've put your pictures away
When your voice has finally left my head
When I've tortured myself with the memories
When I've smoked too many cigarettes
When the circles under my eyes can't get any deeper
When there is no more blood to shed
When I vomit nothing but air
When it is quiet
When I know I am alone
All I can do
is sit
and write it down.

this is not love
========

there is a certain sense
of home, of peace in your arms.
it is not comfort or fulfillment
or a feeling of calm.
it is a cleansing of everything.
something you can only feel
in those unique moments.
This must be like when you
cradle your newborn child in
your arms for the first time and
realize the world has changed.
As if everything in your life was worth it.
All the loss and pain and
what all seemed like an endless
struggle led to
this moment.

And you cannot feel this without
walking through the fire.
Like being carried away and
turned upside down by the tide
struggling to find the surface and
realizing you are about to die
and suddenly feeling the surface of
the water break around your face.
And it is the sweetest breath
you will ever taste.
You gasp at the fresh air and
you've never been so happy to be
blinded by the sun until
bursting up out of
the cold dark water.

This is not love.
This is something else.

It is the first morning that
the drunkard awakes after
his first sober night
that moment of clarity which
only comes after
a lifetime of anguish when
you have what you never wanted
but always needed.
Because it is easier to hate and
to burn down empires than
to forgive and to kneel
before the one who humbled you.

This is not love.
This is
something
else
entirely.

C.R. Andrews

ABOUT THE AUTHOR

C.R. Andrews was born and raised in Chicago, Illinois. He lived there until the age of 28 when he enlisted in the Marine Corps immediately following the attacks of September 11th, 2001. He served for 8 years before being Honorably discharged for disability. He continues to work for the Marine Corps as a civilian and resides in Virginia with 2 3 cats and 1 plant. This is his first publication and has also released his first album entitled "Grapes & Whiskey."

C.R. Andrews

10554502R00058

Printed in Great Britain
by Amazon.co.uk, Ltd.,
Marston Gate.